SKYPE GUIDE

for Grandpas

A Simple Guide To Start Video Chatting with Your Loved Ones

GRANDPATECH .com

Grandparents Quick Guide to Skype
(A simple Guide on Video Chatting with Your Loved Ones)

Table of Contents

Introduction

Skype is currently the most popular video chatting service available to everyone. It's allowed millions of people to connect with each other and bring a rich experience of video chatting to the comfort of your own home.

The other day my mother was able to Skype with her parents and it was beautiful to see how happy they were. It's the closest thing to being there.

Hopefully, by the end of this short, straight to the point ebook, you'll be able to set up and start video chatting your family and friends no matter where they are around the world.

What is Skype?

Skype has been around for over 10 years,

(believe it or not). What started off as a small project has now become the biggest video chatting software in the whole world.

Skype's dominant function is to video & voice call to anyone else who has a Skype account. As long as you have an internet connection you will be able to do this.

Who Uses Skype?

Skype is used by a huge variety of people.

Many people use it to connect with their family and friends overseas. My own family uses it to talk to my grandparents in India.

On the other side of the coin, companies sometimes use Skype to conduct conference calls as you can Skype more than one person at the same time. Companies can also use it to conduct interviews with potential employees.

As you can see, it's application has spread far and wide so it's definitely a good idea to learn how to use it.

Getting Skype on your Computer

Getting Skype on your computer is fairly easy. The process is almost the same regardless of what computer you are using. For simple purposes, I'm going to cover the process of getting Skype on a Mac computer.

Step 1: Go to www.skype.com on your internet browser.
Step 2: Click the Green button in the middle that says 'Download Skype'
Step 3: Next, click the ' Get Skype for Mac' Button on the bottom left of the screen. Skype will then begin to download. Once it finishes downloading, double click the file and drag the Skype icon to your Application Folder.

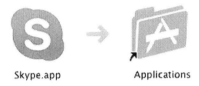

Skype.app   Applications

This will install Skype onto your computer allowing you to start using it.

Getting Skype on your Phone

You can skip this step if you're happy using Skype on your computer only.

Getting Skype on your phone is even easier. It's just an application so just like other applications you'll have to visit the 'app store' or 'play store' depending on whether you have an iPhone or Android.

Once there, search for 'skype' and install the Skype app.

Making an Account

Before being able to Video call anyone you will need to make an account. Making a Skype account has the similar effect to making an email account. Once done, you can give your ID to anyone who you'd like to contact you and begin Skyping with them.

To make an account simply open Skype whether it's on your Computer or Phone and click 'Join us' or 'Create new Account'.

Follow the steps till you have your account ID. Your account ID or 'Skype Username' is your unique ID that, when given to people, will allow them to call or video call you.

Adding Friends

Ok great! You are officially ready to go! At this stage you're ready to being adding your friends so you can Video call them.

To add friends go to Contacts at the top menu and click 'Add Contact' which should be the first option.

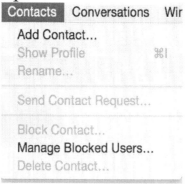

Here, you can simply type in either their Skype username, email address or full name.

Add Contact

Enter the full name, Skype name, or email address of the user you're looking for:

Q˅Search

The easiest way to add someone is to type in their username or email address. Since each person has only one of these, you will only get 1 search result which should be your friend.

If you type in the name, you might get too many search results and you won't know which one is the one you're looking for!

For example, if I type in Joseph Carter, I'll get 100s of results similar to the below,

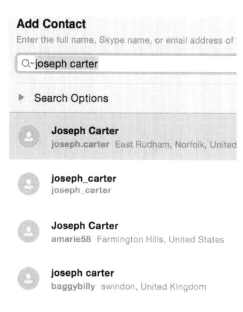

It'll take me forever to find exactly who I'm looking for!

Once you've found who you're looking for either by typing their name, Skype ID or email address, you will need to click the green button that looks like this,

By doing so, you'll send a request to them to be added to their address book. Once they've accepted you're ready to contact each other.

Calling Friends

Skype has many options to contact each other.

You can simply chat message each other by clicking the contact and typing in the text box. You can Voice call each other by clicking the 'Call Phone' button or of course, video call them by clicking the video call button.

Doing any of the 3 above is very simple. Most of you would want to video call so to do that, find your contact or friend that you've just added. He or she should be in the 'contact's' section.

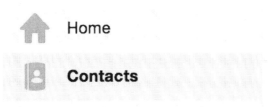

Home

Contacts

Recent

Hover over to their icon picture and a small green button should appear. Click the little arrow on the right side of the button and click 'Video Call'.

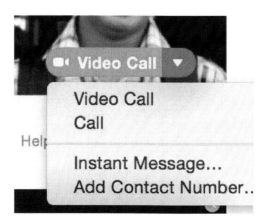

It will now start ringing, just like a telephone does and if they pick up, you'll be able to see them!

Remember, they have to be on the computer or on their mobile phone to be able to see your call coming in. You also have to take into account the time difference as you don't want to be calling your friends over seas in the middle of the night!

It's a good idea let them know in advance that you're going to call them.

Some Skype Tips and Tricks

Calling people who don't have Skype

Now, you can call people who don't have Skype but you'll need call credits for that. Skype has always wanted to make communication free all around the world where possible or at the very least the cheapest it could possibly make it.

For a small price, you can call people overseas, straight on their landlines or mobile phones! To do that, go to 'Home' and click the small dialpad next to search on the top right. It looks like the below,

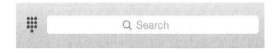

You'll get a small dial pad that will pop up at the bottom left of the screen.

Find the country you want to dial by clicking the drop down and type the number you want to call!

Remember, you will need to have call credits to be able to do this which can be purchased in the 'help' menu of Skype.

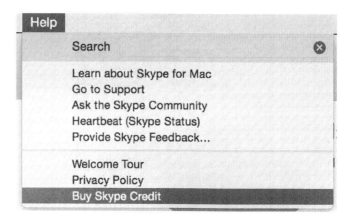

Visit their <u>calling rates</u> page to see the cost of using Skype for overseas calls. It might be cheaper then what you're currently paying.

Sending Files

Skype can be easily used to transfer files such as images and documents between two people. You can send your family some pictures or a document you'd like them to look at.

To do this, simply, double click on your contact till your at the chat screen. At the bottom right of the chat screen you'll see some icons. Click the left icon and find the file you'd like to send.

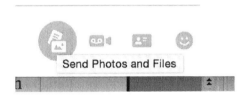

They will need to accept the transfer. Once that's done they can begin downloading the file and will receive it on their end!

8 Ways you Can Use Skype to connect with Family

This book is aimed at seniors wanting to learn Skype. Below is a list of 10 things you can do with Skype,

1. Have a daily conversation over Skype with a friend. You can talk about current or recent events. Things you've read in the newspaper. Basically anything that keeps your mind sharp. It's a bit like meeting up for coffee for a chat with a friend!
2. One of the best things about Skype is that it has let us connect with our loved ones. Tell your grandchildren a nice bed time story before they go to sleep. All they need is someone to set it up on their end and they're ready to go!
3. Have a few rounds of blackjack with a bunch of friends!

4. Play simple games like 'show and tell' with your grandchildren. Ask them what new things they've got recently and I'm sure they won't stop talking about it.
5. Eat dinner or lunch with a friend. Eating time is usually the time family gathers around the table for a conversation about the day and to share a hearty meal together. Why not do the same with Skype?
6. Go through family albums together. If you have any old photos you've found recently and want to share them you can do so over Skype.
7. Allow your children or grandchildren to go through some simple exercises. They can be simple yoga stretches just to get both of your bodies moving.
8. Get someone in the family to Skype you while there's an important event going on. I was at a friends engagement which they held at home and he Skype called his family

overseas so they could watch everything! The whole family were huddled around the family room watching the full ceremony. It was great how everyone could tune in and watch things live.

Ending Remarks

The purpose of this book was to give you a quick overview on how to start Skyping your loved ones. In a couple of weeks, 'Skype Mastery for Grandparents' will be released. Make sure you're part of the Insiders list below so you're notified when it's out!

Click here to join the Insiders List

Skype is a remarkable software and is perfect to connect with our grandchildren. Hopefully this book has served it's purpose in making you more aware of the possibilities of Skype.

I would advise everyone to download it and begin using it. Only through using it continuously will you be comfortable with it.

Good luck and all the best!

- Mateen S